SLIP STREAM

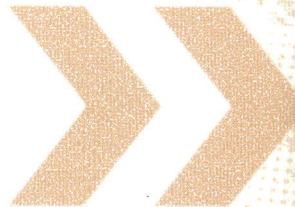

WACKY SPORTS

ANNE ROONEY

FRANKLIN WATTS

LONDON•SYDNEY

Disclaimer – In the preparation of this book, all due care has been exercised with regard to the activities depicted. The Author and Publishers regret that they can accept no liability for any loss or injury sustained.

First published in 2013 by
Franklin Watts
338 Euston Road
London NW1 3BH

Franklin Watts Australia
Level 17/207 Kent Street
Sydney NSW 2000

© Franklin Watts 2013

ISBN 978 1 4451 1953 3

Dewey classification number: 796

A CIP catalogue record for this book is available from the British Library.

Series Editors: Adrian Cole and Jackie Hamley
Series Advisors: Diana Bentley and Dee Reid
Series Designer: Peter Scoulding
Picture Researcher: Diana Morris

Printed in China

Franklin Watts is a division of Hachette Children's Books, an Hachette UK company.
www.hachette.co.uk

Acknowledgements:
Philippa Banks/istockphoto: 19.
Doug Blaine/Rex Features: 8.
Corbis: 15.
epa/Alamy: 16, 17.
Jorg Hackemann/Shutterstock:18.
Hulton Archive/Corbis: 12.
Manit Larpluechai /Dreamstime: 11.
Colin McPherson/Corbis: 23.
Sol Neelman/Corbis: 6.
Erik Pendzich/Rex Features: 4, 5.
Phil Rees/Rex Features: 20.
Rex Features: front cover, 9.
Darren Staples/Corbis: 13.
topten22photo/Shutterstock: 1, 10.
Tim de Waele/Corbis: 14.
Bernd Weissbrod/Corbis: 7.
Peter M Wilson/Alamy: 22.

Every attempt has been made to clear copyright. Should there be any inadvertent omission, please apply to the publisher for rectification.

CONTENTS

WACKY SPORTS

There are all kinds of wacky sports. Wrestling can be an ordinary sport. But some people wrestle dressed as Japanese cartoon characters. That is quite wacky!

Then there are truly wacky sports...

PUMPKIN RACING

Some people make boats out of giant pumpkins. It's not easy to row a pumpkin. The boats are heavy and slimy inside. They also tip over easily!

EXTREME IRONING

Most people don't think of ironing as a sport. But ironing on top of a mountain is wacky. And ironing on top of a moving car is even wackier!

ELEPHANT POLO

Polo players usually ride horses. But in India and Thailand they ride elephants. They need a mallet with a longer handle. This is because an elephant is taller than a horse.

CHEESE ROLLING

In Gloucestershire, UK, people chase a giant cheese rolled down a steep hill. It's fast and dangerous, bouncing over bumps. This wacky race has been run for hundreds of years.

And hundreds of people
have been hurt doing it.

UNDERWATER CYCLING

Why do only one sport at a time? Scuba diving and cycling is really wacky. You need a diving suit, and an air tank so that you can breathe. Don't try it in your local river!'

DUSTBIN RACING

Today many dustbins have wheels. They can be used for dustbin racing. Dustbin racers hurtle around a track. They wear helmets and padding.

Int. Mülltonnenrennen
Hermeskeil

40

H

www.YesAngels.de

ZORBING

A zorb is a giant inflatable ball. Zorb runners get inside the balls and race downhill.

They tumble over and over!

BOG DIVING

Bog divers race along wide, deep ditches.
They often wear wetsuits and snorkels.

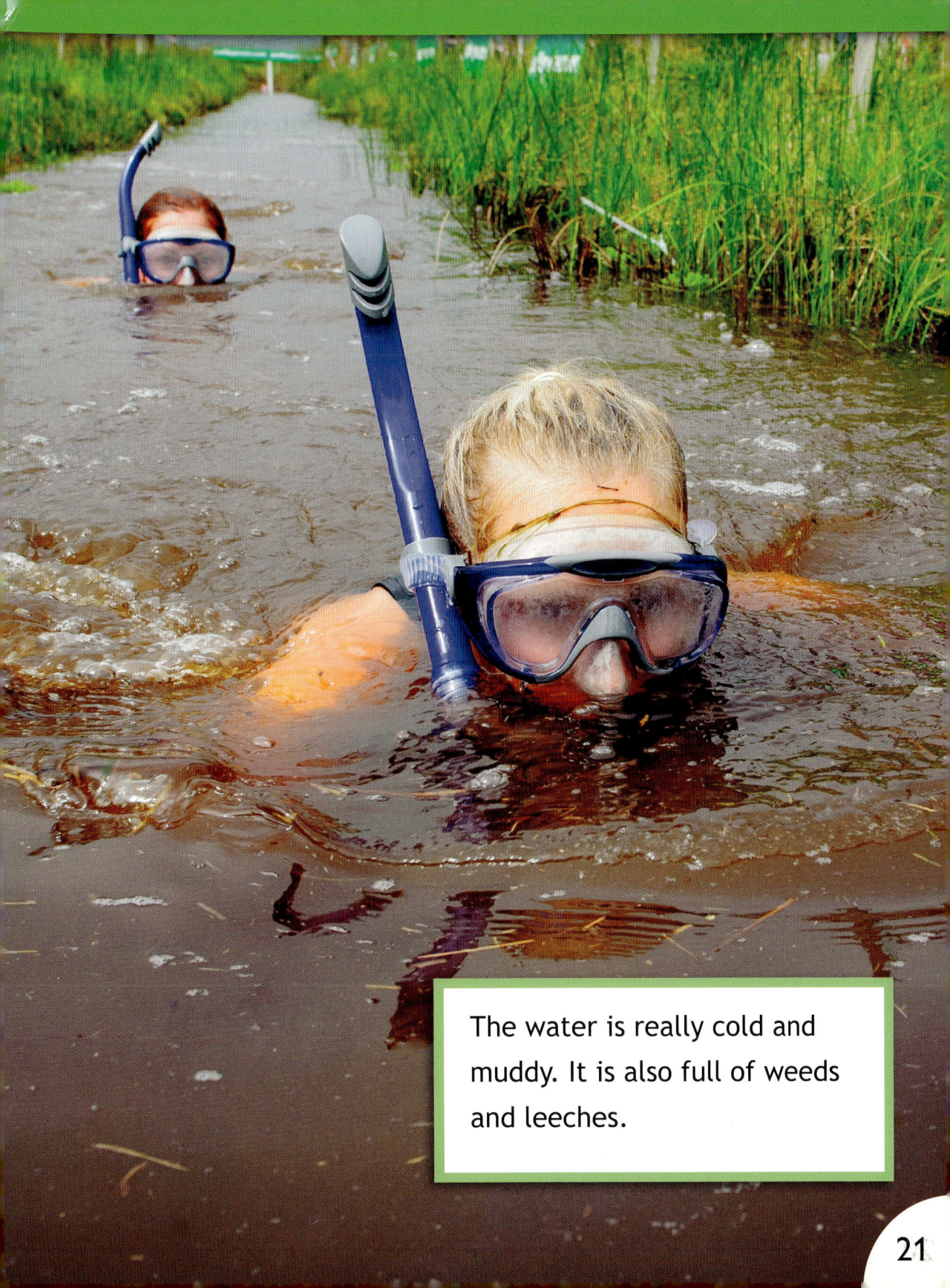

The water is really cold and muddy. It is also full of weeds and leeches.

TRY IT YOURSELF

Some wacky sports are safe to try yourself. Welly-throwing contestants try to throw a boot as far as possible. Don't hit anyone!

Worm charmers race
to catch the most worms.

Can you make up a wacky
sport of your own?

INDEX

FOR TEACHERS

About **SLIPSTREAM**

Slipstream is a series of expertly levelled books designed for pupils who are struggling with reading. Its unique three-strand approach through fiction, graphic fiction and non-fiction gives pupils a rich reading experience that will accelerate their progress and close the reading gap.

At the heart of every Slipstream non-fiction book is exciting information. Easily accessible words and phrases ensure that pupils both decode and comprehend, and the topics really engage older struggling readers.

Whether you're using Slipstream Level 2 for Guided Reading or as an independent read, here are some suggestions:

1. Make each reading session successful. Talk about the text before the pupil starts reading. Introduce any unfamiliar vocabulary.

2. Encourage the pupil to talk about the book using a range of open questions. For example, what is the wackiest sport or activity they can think of?

3. Discuss the differences between reading non-fiction, fiction and graphic fiction. What do they prefer?

For guidance, SLIPSTREAM Level 2 – Wacky Sports has been approximately measured to:

National Curriculum Level: 2b
Reading Age: 7.6–8.0
Book Band: Purple

ATOS: 2.4*
Guided Reading Level: I
Lexile® Measure (confirmed): 540L

*Please check actual Accelerated Reader™ book level and quiz availability at www.arbookfind.co.uk

Slipstream Level 2 photocopiable **WORKBOOK**
ISBN: 978 1 4451 1797 3
available – download free sample worksheets from:
www.franklinwatts.co.uk